THE POST-AMERICAN CULTURAL CONGRESS

to my mother and father

THE POST-AMERICAN CULTURAL CONGRESS

Sam Abrams

THE BOBBS-MERRILL COMPANY, INC.

INDIANAPOLIS • NEW YORK

NOTE TO READER. Almost all these poems can only be read aloud. S. A.

ISBN 0-672-51250-5 Hardcover
ISBN 0-672-51927-5 Paperback
Library of Congress Catalog Card Number 73-16810
Designed by Helga Maass
Manufactured in the United States of America

First printing

CONTENTS

The Nature of my Work is Visionary or Imaginative; it is an Endeavor to Restore what the Ancients called the Golden Age.

SONG BY WAY OF A PROLOG/
8 DAYS OF THE WEEK

i burn within heart's anger
ask forgiveness
like no wise man
(   ) i dont want nothing
love is impossible enough
meaning slips away from language
sing or dance in sun or dark
(   ) or just dont do nothing
ask me no questions
tell you nothing
pleasure is absence of pain
(   ) just dont say nothing
look   the hand becomes a   hand
love is impossible enough
pleasure is absence of pain
(   ) dont ask for nothing
sing or dance
give what you have
(   ) i dont want nothing

SATURDAY

crazy   mixed
up   dick
you   can
now   can
you   boast

i am at a loss i
have nothing but
poetry

nothing but poetry a
program for players
                why

is there nothing
& not something

sundayfatherdayfatherstdayneardayheredayrealdayfeelday
but satur   day
a mixture   satyr
a tzimis of goat & man

nothing but poetry
sustains this monster

everyone is staring at us
in this scary 1/2
deserted city

SUNDAY

corn king
1/2 crazy old maid & a
professor throwing
knives at trees "he
could cut a throat at 20 paces"

3 days 7 i sit
in my study there is
no rhythm i have in common with these people
we go in different
directions "the stairway
in the dew the footsteps
shine" but who's to go
thru the snow with these nuts

from every shire's end
up the pike to ski
country it is

the best we have it seems
the young as brightly as
anything

MONDAY

i
am a much better poet
than lover this is
no boast

these
girls are hot after their
own fashions
but i
need learned hands & subtle
mountains

i
have established themes which
will continue my
truths & lies have
become my past

i cannot talk with these
crazy people & the sane ones
do not talk to me
we understand one another

WEDNESDAY

on wednesday we made love not war
on wednesday we made the working class
who are always less self-delusory
than the bushwazee

on wednesday we made marks on papers
on wednesday we made judgment
on wednesday we gave advice

go buy a car   read
play until you are 30
have fun   stretch your

on wednesday we were afraid
on wednesday we watched the beloved iceskater on peacock
        pond
on wednesday we gave what gifts we could

FRIDAY

on friday taunton massachusetts is an inland city

the river runs
the silly damn river
does not know

on friday taunton massachusetts is an inland city

the last of the multimasted schooners was built
frozen fish ugly goose up
coast & down gothick our monuments

we reel thru the streets of taunton massachusetts

kicking jack williams what shall we do
shall we freeze our own guts
for the sake of these crazy people

for kit & philip

LIKING CHILDREN

a wish for some occasion

live hapiLy
AND love

a house
or an airplane with one wing
longer than the other

making a sky blue with
crayons on that rough paper
& meet green grass

i know what i am talking about

with or without
equally impossible

i know what i am talking about

a wish for some occasion
live hapiLy
AND love

SONG FOR SOME SAD KID

is already written
i can
say nothing understandable

growl or whine
the fur is on the backs of my hands
as i type these lines

a figure of fable
the selfrighteous what
beast deserves my
cowardly frivolity

my teeth would crack
before the softest nut

the prehensile tongue
wraps round the earthworm
sucked down my throat
american

virginibus puerisque

WEDNESDAY/2

i am asking you to listen
to what i know not
what i am say i am asking
you   to listen

i thought i saw a 3rd eye staring at me
in the forehead of the yellow man who
sweeps even your steps

i put the properties of numbers
between the eye in the crocus
& my eye

separation is painfull repetition
repetition   repetition
in itself is painfull

LOVE ON A PLATTER

"i do not have a simple spirit
but the rancorous heart of a child"

hear real sounds only
i would laugh to hear you
crying going away

i dont need nobody
cause i only wanna be loved
(   ) all the time

FRAGMENT

to go down on all fours
& bite the ground & howl
& run before the hounds
& wear a skin grey as the heart
within my breast lady it is not
hard to do this for you

where ere i walk cool
breezes fan the air   i can
not stop shaking   i am
not afraid

RC COLA

a horse seen by you
a horse seen by me
cannot stand
for the samething

while you have dreamt
or haven't
i pay off old debts

in mem WCW

PRIVATE SPEAKING

as if after a stroke
with difficulty not
lack of control

but astonished   beside
oneself   with difficulty
moving lips as if

of another   tell him
to speak   to get up
to take your hand

tell him to feel
your hand that he
has taken in his

———

tell him it is warm
it moves when you
least expect it to move

or does not when
you do whatever it is
you must do

he is astonished he
cannot talk
fast enough

NO TITLE

to escape from
   categories
      the wish is not enough

i have neglected
   many things
   my hand
is unformed   how
can a soft bellied man
   be a father

one has no right to
be more ugly than is necessary
how many children have died
that i might smoke
smoke my cigarette

where's rhetoric
why lie when it is harder
to tell the truth

repeat

no poem but the world

no escape from "form"

THE LAW OF ISTHMUSES

the opposite of fear is not courage but desire
heavenly aphrodite oldest of those three whom men call fates
honor & fear & greed & the greatest of these is the first
was said in an age really less degenerate than ours
yet the third tried to take what was not to be taken
& cut across the isthmus of megara to the west
& even carthage was not out of their calculations
to conquer the city of merchants with never a poet
not even god save the mark a politician to boast of
is the ambition correctly called fatal
successful or not it rarely misses its mark
& alcibiades was also the most beautiful man of his day
& those were the quick eye & the true mouth gone under
in the quarries of syracuse as in the paddies of asia
in the streets of the city as in the sands of the arena
& i wish i cd say with the saint
those who with an avid thirst to cure their mortal ill
drank from the fresh slit jugular vein the blood flowing
     still warm

where are they now
ubi   sunt

these are my fathers
these are my wishes
desire & fear
are with me now

LAW OF THE JUNGLE

& their greatest man was a general
salt was sowed on the wound
yet no individual

my waking hours are troubled
my minutes are fragrant
by people burning in far off flooded fields
in tunnels cut in the earth
we found on the wall an inscription

the smoke of my cigarette is the smell of burning flesh
which may be injurious to your health
burning with fear is the same as burning with desire
our daily television transmits metaphors
into my bedroom the face of a talking dog
records! records! for what company
more news
my son says goodnight to walter cronkite
the hell sound
the mo   town sound

THE LAW OF POVERTY

exemplum salutis publicae cives posuere

the house sparrows turn golden in the late sun
the full moon where's his goat mask
who is you is i wingless but political
animals with habits

give a cigar with a tip to the wounded man

one must take up what's before one's hands
how to make these fools stop interfering
with my love life

I will not put a structure on it
throw out my neckties
as part of responsibility to my sons

in the 30th year of my age
i stopped from blind admiration for pericles
hate fills the interstices in the mind
between love & poetry
hate fills my african friends
hate fills my pockets

i have an automobile 2000 or so books paintings a persian
    carpet

i have laid this exile on my self

love is all
to found community

THE LAW OF POVERTY/2

i propose mortification of observation how
ever little is not necessary willows
only seem to turn yellower in spring light
& osiers redder

the fashion for jewish crackpots
vs. catholic
has much to do with this foolishness

i propose the memory of baron corvo
who was not ashamed
flew kites in spring air
understood the opposites
philosophy or therapy
desire is fearless

for ezra

BLUE LAW

please her amoral or mystical
charge & damn yr truth
lady if joy is only
absence of pain

chemical accidents complicate
benvenuto cellini musician
smith son fighter
too fond of truth carved
from ivory or wood a toy unfit
for a gentleman

for recreation   for recreation
to take it up occasionally
for recreation   & play as
once you played for
obedience' sake

DANCE BY WAY OF AN EPILOG/
MAYDAY 1966

*is become a call
of distress dance
communication too
sex love & laughter
art even in birds
who are dumber
than they look*

*pair of doves livia livia
pair of herring gulls
do almost the same dance
in the air between
the verrazano bridge
& the water*

*"it serves
to strengthen the pair bond*

*gull (larus) has been known
to overrespond to artificial
super stimuli*

*jets are mistaken for hawks
in the swamp at norton*

*may day 1966 is
become a call
of distress jets
are taken for hawks
picnickers & president
in the same basket
fouler or fairer red
is the color
of all men's blood*

dance while
cause you can
to meet death

all orders & phyla
tribes of birds
hot blooded whales
serpo still in repose
flying insects of the air
crawling insects of the mold
porky pig &
woody guthrie sick
white politicians
my 2 sons
workers of the world
outdoor fucking
walk on grass
may
may
day

to here: THE BOOK OF DAYS

LETTERS FROM URBANA 6

cant do better than Bama
threatened Alberta in the
L of C mikes

but cant do better   tho
whiskey when i'm dry   yet
baby when i need you

dont socio on me   put out
for winos   tho the point exactly
they're sweet
for it

just in brooklyn jump
for me in the morning   a little
before light & it's ok
make me a liar

not much   steal toady lie
suckd my cock   youth   yet   look
around   i know honor & love
more than most

MARCH 61

soon as rain lets up a little
damnd cardinal starts whistling
what good does it do
to talk to women
lovely poems
if only they wdnt make such a deal
outta not doin it like men
doing it only for love

i'm afraid the squirrels will
jump down on me out of the trees

i'd forgive you
knowing me
but feel bad
more than i expect you
probably less than you'd feel

talk about how i am i'd do
think me a shmuck? think i do
not keeping shut up
like you

i almost threw up this morning
          sun after shower
at the smell of the fertility of the earth

GOT OUTTA BED TO REMEMBER

whether he got em
holding up her arse
or they fell asleep
later together
the sores on the backs
of his hands
that wdn't heal
i've never been as heroic as I . .

which isn't to say
i don't love as much
or more
or better

(for G)

HEARTS AT THE BEACH

how can you tell if
the tide's going in or out
bay 2 fags keep steppin
on the piece of reed
i stuck in the sand for a dead line

y' cant slap the cards on a blanket
& it ruins the game
(my grandma taught me
when i had the mumps
i watched the old retired men
in the park
whoppin the cards
on the cement tables

all gulls look ragged close up
worse when they're young
before their marks are clear on 'em
not sea gulls either
millions in the tall grass
on the plains   i've not seen

wet wind's foggin glasses
sweatshirt sticks
cards wont shuffle

———————

brought gin every day
wives brown
2 new bathing suits
meeting D with her mex cigarettes
your fatigue cap

whatever happened to your fatigue cap

---

once i askd shd i dedicate
to who i love or hate
& walked an hour by the water
making up a peace
looking down bathing suits
finally preferring young mothers
      the season's over
but tits dont freeze
it's cold this winter
but reason has tits
      you can only kill a man with a gun
but you can whittle with a tit
when you got nothing better to do

& cold at nights
2 families alone
sand flies biting

                !

well met black gull

fare well seas

i done you wrong my seas

i hear you calling
some other daddy's name

HEADS   BONES

1st time in the new year
walkin to school
think of G. . . & S. . . .

unprep more as a teacher than student
inept lifer cant protect self
from jockers nor screws

my friends are sulking in their tents
moon in the morning casts nothing on the snow

you cwazy wabbits! the condemned man
(got nothing better to do)
sings on his heart klea andron

LIKE A PRO

the best man on his way
from work brings flowers
to his wife & kids

wild or buy at 42nd street
can find in january

a definition of courage intelligence
from hector and others

WHITE FANG

poets
have been
had & will be
again by these
men

ishalright
th besht
don fight
   & mosht lovely

THE PAST SPRING IS
THE SAME AS THE COMING

i hate 1/2faded flowers
throw 'm out as soon as they
begin to wilt

the flowers on this desk
are in a jar with
markings on its sides
cup   1/2   cup   1/4   cup

hedge! buddy hedge!
dont let it get you down
cup   1/2   cup   1/4
faded   faded

THE PACIFIC GOLDEN PLOVER

flies over 2000 miles
over water
from alaska to hawaii

& the artic tern has
sunshine all day
all night
8 months of the year
near both poles

"we move these old chairs
from room to room"

my dear my dear
in the great american desert
there's a swift ("that tireless oarsman!")
that hibernates
in dusty caves

over 2000 miles
of course in the
spring too

PREDICATIVE POSITION

with last night's
make up not washd
  off in Widener
gang bangs
gang bangs
  Oh Saturday!
  morning!
so many rhythms fall
on dead (p.p.) ears

(for Eric W)

XEINE PATER

i do not touch
a guide to safe
conduct but
a poor one

athena assume your disguise
tho it be to call me sir
i will yet in nature's despite
even grow older

CENTO

some say an army on horses
   i'm alabama bound
some foot others a fleet
   on this black earth
   i'm alabama bound
the fairest thing but   i   she
whoever one loves
   don cha leave me here

i can't love no
immortal Aphrodite throned in charm
one woman at a time
daughter of Zeus trickster
i always got   6   7   8   standin in line
   i pray you
master not my heart lady
with pain   and sorrow
don
      cha
         leave
               me
                  here

CITY MOUSE

i am assaulted
on all sides by
shrill noises
beauty   sex
call it what
you will

———————

what can you
say about
fire
burning in
fireplace
nothing
to do but
watch it poke
now
then   add a log

unless something
drive you
to the typewriter say
or bed   or
to listen for bird calls

i am assaulted
on all sides
behind my chair
there   is nothing

WCW WLD'VE LIKED
THE PROF OF ECOLOGY

bull briar shall be my plant
"damn thing" its leaves in fall
are darkly marked by veins against
the yellow   one of the things of this land
that fought the farmers   now in this
old part of the federation   has taken back
the fields   european greenbriar   flowers
fits in ballads & graveyards   but no one
in his right mind wd cultivate
bull briar "damn thing"

I CAN'T EVEN DRINK YOUR WATER

the colors   the day   the motions
how many times have i said
come see the day before if goes
thell never be a day like this again
        (the road by the shed in the west light
        the red tree at the end of the river road
        the white of this paper
        & on it the shadow of my head

        when the whistle from the factory blew
        a dozen song sparrows flew
        out of the tangle around me

not one of all these leaves perfect   not one
not bit by caterpillar or gall   not one
of eleven hundred girls
walking in these woods   today

BLESS'M ALL

praise of the persistence
of desire of no less
"the fat legs
of the local girls
dancing with each other" it
in heres

no less in her own
bony arse m' dear
this too must cheer
& raise my heart

no less in   mere
words   "a girl in
a bikini   "in images
in age   in years
we pass
dear no less

this too:
i cld not you
if not
them all

10 DEC 64

DAME EDITH SITWELL POET DIES
TODAY tall as a crane & twice
as creaky tall as a genie
her gifts surround us yet

the bark & bite of yaller dogs
turns to fawns on death's sight
who described the pet
after the raid at the kibbutz
what he had in his mouth was
a bloody kotex

i suppose the occasion forgives
those who greet life with cries
or silence & death with
pictures and solecistic loveliness

queer & voted to frivolity
i owe her some of my basic seriousness

THE ONE EYED MAN IN THE COUNTRY

who are yet young
& have not tasted
of evils

are ours to hold
in rooms in dormitories
by 1/2 past 10

are ours not to touch
not ass with mind
nor soul with hand

nothing is lovelier
than an ice storm
a young girl or man

is like a cat
or owl or any
unblinking thing

———————

who cannot see
what is real because
they are real

are here as i am
not nor will be
again ever

are here to touch &
not be touched
nor see

*my world smaller
& more vast curiously
more detailed*

————

*a puppy eats more
than a dog but both
like to play
in the snow*

NOVA LOCAL

we fuck not often
enuf for pleasure but
enuf for love

last night
i saw the new moon
with the old moon in her arms

& heard nothing &
saw nothing but moon & stars

dog shit & a carburetor
in our back yard no flowers
in our house either
scribbling on the walls

after apollinaire

GRANDPRÉ

here asters the color of your shadowed eyes

flower
leaning to violet like their shadow & this autumn
& my life poisoning itself on your shadowed eyes

kids come from school with noises
dressed in jumpers playing harmonica
they pick asters here like mothers
daughters of their daughters like your eyelids
which beat like flowers beating in a mad wind

regardless of all this la he sings very gently
just as slow & mooing these cattle move
for once all from this great meadow

A SONNET ASSONNET FOR FEE

dull days like this there are
to see only black birds
in spite of all oddly blooming
at once early & late
we insult our athletes
repeatedly yet for formality
's sake repetition of formality
to be precise they play

resemblance to a flower
any natural thing cannot be
accidental herodotus said
dice were invented to allay
hunger pains & coke of course
in a sense a dance

SONNET FOR TIM REYNOLDS
AND MY SHADOW

dull in this particular droughty spring
overrun by sun water rich of flowering
earth to see sea waves raised against us

let's take a motor bike to the south
or west run 100 balls go climb a tree
which is not the climbing tree

remains dull days unleashed against
children of our minds
against the astronomical spaces

elaborately calculate the source
of what according to the cold enemy
are messages

if spring come can winter
if body can mind

"indifferent as to the sources"

we cd & ought
to stay down here
& be warm the woods
are wet the moon
is shining just as whitely
here

poet nachus already
ive met fucked
& written you a poem
i know yr name better
than i know my own

to hell with apt quotation with

apt anything "the
fitting" in this or that let's
do what does
      can not be
fitting in construct memory or
even to create its
own only simple
action

the hand becomes a flower like
look the hand becomes a flower
without value intention meaning
is a category that does not always
apply

COUNTERSHADING

The artist, by the skillful use of light and shade, produces in two dimensions the illusory appearance of roundness; nature, on the other hand, by the skillful use of counter-shading produces in three dimensions the illusory appearance of flatness.

I. classical equivalents

eros . . . . . cupid   ity amor   al
it translates then to cash
& a mooning i.e. holding his
flat face towards it in the day
brown & white bull in an overgrazed
field shielded by the trees mrs ames
benefacted the town

from dirty books & cheapie
but legal films to come
to this

a girl picking flowers in a field

reason enough for the earth to open
and all things die

II. our lady of purgatory

yet then she was
a girl picking flowers in a field
in that fertile island
she was a girl in all
innocence with friends
the grass knee high & higher

no one ever said otherwise
who have put unicorns battles
in "sward" you name it no
one makes that mistake among
the unmown corn then or
corn's wild ancestor knee high
high as that famous & valentine
shaped arse then she was a girl
picking flowers the earth opened
our lady of purgatory

III. cutflowers

screaming but not those
in those days she sang
a girl gathering days
of many colors

of many colors

bunched against her breast
held with the whole right arm

her left relaxed hanging
turned from the elbow
to show us her open palm

vel ibyci opera omnia fidelissime translata

THE FAMOUS NAME OF ORPHEUS

(I)
always   *ah*
always   *like that swift*
        that narrow winged
        purple bird

when

there   on the tops of the rocks
sit shining   shining forgetful
the sea birds
the long wing halcyons

like not like
you at all i
feel desire i

(II)
myrtle violet goldtwist
apple rose curling laurel

flames which thru the night
shining threads

it isn't possible for the dead
to find a cure for life

(III)
wide eyed case of desire
stung the hair the daughter
of property of
posterity

the peaks from which
we choose to fight

sea grace pale grey daughter
long hair bent over the cradle
love gently persuasion
raised you among roses

second dance/for the summer solstice

the dance of words
the only word for
10 years   coney island whitefish
was what a joke for

10 years scumbags
float mouth up
in ny harbor

in noork will dance
manday morning hop fribble
true the streets with eyes
tin symbol by the road side
in the headlights unless
it move

the news key to kelly's symbol
lying by the road side

a responsible poetry

answer the telephone
answer me

———

solly & manny standing still
corner of 10th & 2nd
benthetic hunters long points
extended eyestalks
for the blind fish the organic rain

scum bags float
always mout up
in my harbor

eyes shine
by the side of the road
in reflected light

lotor lotor
moved by spring
"the tree is a nutmeg"
the blind fish

a poetry for tompkins square
a poetry for milton massachusetts
rather than community
a clean stream
better than love
a nutmeg tree

scum bags their only name
float mouth up
in ny harbor

lotor lotor wash us clean
draco volans fly with us

2nd stage/in praise of barbara

an argument against poetry
these feelings persist new
seeming until i need
records of my past
no (new) feelings "he
    ceased to grow
to have a
      subject

only the records
himself
object but not artifact
a mess mesa raised
table tabula rasa
  a rats bed & board

buried her baby
alive at least
    no release
for this at least
i have not let
my face be used

for jw & ba

know no other love than that you teach
can sing circuses triple thrown ac
dc with pirouette on the return

let all bridges fly no heart
fill sky but completes man

the wind blows across the lake
manuscripts blocks of hash may it
tonite bring you what you need
hawkins in the street old man

(Washington Square 28 Oct 66)

EPINIKION

BALLPOINT or typewriter
bombshape or rocket
arrowclipt in the pocket alike
of marine or shoe clerk

A VICTORY SONG

for those who carry   not even one pen
without pockets over their hard soft
breasts no room to put anything in
the pockets stretched over narrow
arses a song for those we have not yet
unmanned totally those yet not without all grace

the abiding glory of this competition
the abiding glory of this laughter
laughter under unseasonal sun shadow
of the 1st electric lightsign
competition with laughter to win
laughing to try all of your powers with no
strain balance on one leg tight pants pick up
the token jump & turn in air red stripes tight
pants boots blond hair black skin olive skin
like milk 3 girls "it is called hopscotch"
a dance among the houses of heaven
chalk lines the black top chalk make an
order of chaos as all creation defines
the obscure kosmos becomes

light steps turn in air you dance the discovery
of america may it be

———————————

a possession for your children
chalk in large sticks sold
only at halloween only by
candy stores pastel colors
to draw the goblins which will frighten away the dead
you need a sidewalk washed every day
the merchant his white apron
the broom that licences the young
once a year to draw on this sidewalk these windows
the children will protect us
with the signs they know
among ourselves we tried to mark one another
get the spot between the shoulder blades
cover a hand with chalk slap
orange was best red hardest to get out
blue did not show up on the dark mackinaws of my days

mark for the dead
take him
not me

also we disguised ourselves
collect our protection money

their faces almost gone from my memory
poets only offer the same kind of totally unsatisfying
                                        immortality
pen & chalk 1926 carved in the beech
everything is down there waiting for the excavator

———————————

break a hole in the city walls
like they say a fairy land dad bag
on the hudson float americas out
after twosies after threesies whoeverwins i got bored altho
                                        wisdom

is mightier there are
more pretty girls than you can shake
8 pretty mothers on a bench
one i saw breaking her daughter

the dance on the black top
under which no thing awaits
bones removed to potters field
elm under which the militia exercised is looking sick
arch has been cleaned

let us erect a standard
dance on the black top over earth

———————

for these girls many men with
cocks arched high with desire with going to your utmost
without strain to compete among one another
laughing to sit on the black top without getting dirty
    their grace
        for us
            for their children

SUNFLOWERS

My memories are confused haploid
diploid once a foodplant of importance
in the drought season when ever
conditions are hard these weeds
flourish in fact defined by hard times

as early as 1822 the 8th millennium bc
the international community of campfollowers
across which the bankers on clear days can see but not be seen

there may be an american art
there may be an american poetry
never in new jersey

in paterson a state of not mind a state
of feeling does not flourish in these airs these
waters without any dissolved oxygen at all this land of
weed community and rare birds

to colonize disturbed land
on the banks of a tributary of the amazon
as well as east 10th street

to turn our faces to the sun

these factories
weary of the mundane
sit upon a branch & sing of no interest no birth
past the stagnant waters where the powerless souls of the
                                        dead sing weakly
the phoebe snow will run for the last time on the 10th

THE POSSIBILITY
OF A FAIR EXCHANGE IS

a gift as lovely for a birth
as for a marriage

at 36 it's all in the family
& he it came to pass
in spite of all he
did not sacrifice
his son
    the impossible
happens every day this
is the east side love
comes to the most impossible people
sons are born the sun rises
meteors fall tho they are not seen
civilization endures some how even
happiness

each man gets
better than he deserves
old lech old drunk the
bird sings at morning
for sake of the song

after Aragon

LAMENT FOR THE PRIDE OF BARBARISM

stopped by explosive they come back
by daylight tired crazy rage come back
by day women bend men resemble
cursewords women bend cry lost toys
children open large eyes

cry lost toys children no understanding
horizon badly defended children watch no understanding
machine gun on the corner

machine gun soldiers talk quietly count
wounded & dead girl friends say home o
love girl friends sleep with their snapshots
the sky outlives the swallows

sleep with their pictures on stretchers
of unbleached canvas to be buried on stretchers
young people are being carried red
mouth grey skin young people

who knows what use the enemy
tanks have cut off the sea
between us what shall they find there
the enemy tanks that our sins be
forgiven us

passerby
> *he was black as the bombs*
> *a giant returning*
> *for better or worse*
> *a 1000 times better*
> *to be shot at home*

than go away
a 1000 times better
to die at home

here we go home here we go home
no more tears no more hope no more guns
the people who live in peace over there
sent us their cops
the people who live in peace over there
sent us under their bombs
there is no way thru
we're going back
no need to dig our graves
we're going back
with our wives & kids
no need to ask for mercy
with wives & kids
saint christophers of the highway
giants outlined
without even a club in hand
the giants under a sky white with anger

rimbaud

MAY FLAGS

contrast beech branches hello dies while
spirituals flutter in the bushes that
our blood sing in our veins
brambles twist sky blue like
an angle blue touches wave
i'm going if sunlight wound me
i'll die on grass

patience bored too
fucking simple fuck my worries
let summer dramatic ties
me to fortune care for
you for nature to
die less alone
less nothing where the workers
die hilarious in the world

i'd really like the seasons to use me
to you nature i give me
my thirst & my hunger
if you'd like nurse i
have no illusions
laugh at sun laugh at one's parents
me i don wanna laugh at nothing
free this bad luck

neruda

NO MORE

with truth aligned to
install light on earth

wanted to be like bread
struggle didn't find me missing

but here i am with what i love
with solitude which i lost
joined to that rock no rest

the sea works in my silence

EPIGRAMS OF PLATO

I. DAKRUA MEN HEKABE

tears for Hecuba and for the Trojan women
  the fates spun out in those days
for you Dio having won a victory of fair deeds
  the gods have poured out wide hopes
you lie in your broadplained homeland honored by the
    citizens
  O thou who drove my heart mad with love Dio

II. AION PANTA FEREI

What are the attributes of the power of time, who knows
    how
to change, so easily and quickly, a man's name and face and
body and fortune?

I am the irresistible power of time, destroyer of cities,
Kali who dances, Kali who wears a garland of skulls, Kali
of the resplendent body, Kali who dwells near at hand.

III. NAUEGOU TAPHOS

what did the deep sea say
tell me what did the deep sea say
it moaned & it groaned & it splashed & foamed
& rolled on its weary way

IV. PLOTERES SOZIOSTHE

a beautiful rose every day
i place on the crest of the waves
said take it please & let the petals fall
above his watery grave

APOLLINAIRE'S ANNIE

on the sea coast of Texas
between Mobile & Galveston there is
a big garden all roses
& also within a house
which is a big rose

a woman walks
in the garden alone
& when i go by on the lime
shaded road
we look at one another

since she is a sunmason
her roses & her clothes
dont have any buttons
2 are missing from my coat
we practise almost the same religions

THEOGNIS OF MEGARA

REJOICE WITH ME MY HEART
SOON OTHER MEN WILL LIVE BUT I
SHALL BE DEAD AND BLACK EARTH

IT WAS SAPPHO
WHO FIRST COMPARED A BRIDE
TO AN APPLE

like the sweet apple reddening on the tip of the branch
on the tip of the highest branch the pickers forgot
no they have not forgot but they coud not reach

like the hyacinth in the mountains the shepherds tred
under foot and on the ground the purple flower

diogenes laertius

THE HEGESIANS

what makes grandma love ole granpa so
what makes grandma love ole granpa so
he can still do the boogy like he did 40 years ago

the so called hegesians believe
  in the same goals
  pleasure and pain
that neither gratitude
  nor friendship
  nor beneficence
  exist
  as they are never
  chosen for themselves
  but because of personal needs
  in the absence of which
  they would not exist
that happiness cannot possibly be
  for the body is full of affects
  and together with the body
  the soul
  must feel
  and be upset
  chance forbids much that is expected
  so for these reasons
  happiness is nonexistent
and they maintain that
  there is nothing
  naturally pleasant
  or unpleasant
  but that thru want

  or familiarity
  or surfeit
  some men are pleased
  some are not
they take no account of
  poverty or wealth
  in regard to happiness
  for rich men and poor men
  take pleasure no differently
the state of slavery is equally
  no limit of pleasure
  opposed to freedom
  nor noble birth
  against low
  nor fame
  against obscurity
that life is profit for a fool
  indifferent to a wise man
that the wise man always acts
  for his own sake
  for there is no one
  worth as much
  even if
  he expect to reap
  the greatest benefits
  from someone
  it would not be equivalent
  to what
  he would provide to himself
they disown the senses
  on the grounds that
  they do not make exact
  knowledge
that one should do all
  that appears reasonable
they say that wrong actions
  should be forgiven

for no one does wrong
willingly but
under the compulsion
of some affect
and not to hate
but rather to instruct
the wise man does not thus
benefit from his wisdom
in selection of goods
as in avoidance
of evils
making it his aim
to live without pain
and without worry
which benefit accrues
to those who do not distinguish
between the sources of pleasure

BUT WE HAD NO PERICLES

icicles dont hang from my eves
bookies sell them on bicycles
strait sociology again
from my golden ironies   or or or

or o a cry of amazement the possibilities
were golden we let lampreys upon
black rat
rifle barbed wire poison bait the
STEEL TRAP sandbags dykes deforest
tear up the sod which held the land down
damned up flood of mississippi
that covered the earth with
MUD we sweep into
our mississippi
                    beaver
                        bear
                            buffalo
the gentle native pigeon
                        both eagles
sometimes a buzzard as far east as the bronx
green paraqueet diamond jims shad
            the alewife "a fish
of little commercial importance such & such
creatures the
                league of the 5 nations
                the 3 civilized tribes
                the cities of the south
each of us has a story who
survives into adulthood "breeding condition
in 1967 in this united states
some stroke of luck known or
unknown

VIETNAMESE LIFE PROJECT

only one subject i
return again & again i
sit at a typewriter &

put my hand to
create a new civilization
it is not hard

to understand
pound turned to fascism
eliot to   o eliot

only the one i
light a cigarette
describe vietnamese

life
a fair sample
a giant crossbow to

shoot down copters
snakes hung in a tunnel
against the advance of empire

hither spain or further
carthage or rome
some say
the fairest thing on this black earth

chariot or flashing foot
clippership under sail but i
say it is she whoever
one loves

1 1/2

my friends stand up bitter
taste of this country on their
faces of mankind still
a monster animal
grace hidden all
wearing barbarian pants
short hair mark of slave
or prussian

a narrative preoccupation politics
creep into everyone's poetry the
reputation of the spotted hyena
is being rehabilitated you son
of a bitch you are so beautiful how
have you managed to fuck up
so many things

the shit is thoroughly mixed in
with the sand beachcombing is an honorable
profession   on all coasts
solitary men with shovel & sack
pieces of screen baskets salvage
what they can small change lost
on crowded hot afternoons

the wall is needed to keep the
sand from returning to the sea
the fence is needed to keep
people from injuring themselves
play ball only in designated areas

every 7 years roughly
the lemming cycle hence
gyrfalcons & the snowy owl

a "heap of dirty laundry
great flights late november to january
'60 '67 vicinity of garbage dumps &
beaches it is supposed that
the majority never make it back

PARRHASIUS' UNOBJECTIONABLE BOAST

I

even tho i speak to
those who
listen without belief
i say that i claim
the clear ends of this art have been found
by me an insurmountable boundry
has been set
tho men get no thing perfect

II

say i bullshit
             you may
                       let it go
framed & tied art's
                   terra
                        firmata
                              & clarity
man's faction
              fiction without purple
                                    deep ends
ours a moment
             sudden agent
                          over buoys

ALARIC

Alaric (c. 370-410), chief of the Visigoths from 395 to his death, conqueror of Rome. (Encyclopaedia Britannica)

Alaric al arik Gothic King and conqueror; (Encyclopedia Americana)

He's not mentioned at all in Heichelman & Yeo, History of the Roman People *(Prentice Hall, 1962, intended & heavily promoted as a college text,) nor in the usually very good* Oxford Companion to Classical History. *Starr has the good sense (thank God! I know the man.) to at least mention the sack of Rome in his* History of the Ancient World. *Scramuzza & McKendrick,* The Ancient World *(Holt, 1958, the best college text) give it a pretty good paragraph, though they should have referred the student to Gibbon's great set piece on the sack (Ch. XXXI) which is the ultimate source of their paragraph. Rostovtzeff,* Rome *(a reprint of Vol. 2 of his* Social and Economic History of the Ancient World) *does not mention the sack at all. Rostovtzeff's is the most influential and widely used college textbook of Roman history.*

The 2 obvious reasons for the cover-up: fear that it's gonna happen here as it must, and cause, since we beat the indians, it's important to be able to believe that the winners are the good guys. so . . .

"however rugged or self reliant the individual Iroquois or Algonquin, Bushman or Zulu — however superior in many features his sensory and mental organization — his loosely knit society has been destroyed or absorbed by the closely knit units of some dominant people wherever there has been serious competition." (C. P. Haskins, Of Men & Societies)

SIRVENTES: THE ACCIDENT
OF THE GUN

arrival at the tip of africa
50 years too soon
                    cause some hittite
someone in hittite territory
learned how
            to make iron swords
            to use the horse in
such a way
            single inventions made
as it happens here or there or
rather one invention
on the coast of asia minor by semite
                            or greek
accident of geography
                    epistemology &
dont let em tell you
                science does work is
even beautiful
            that mess of
colonial fucking administrators
drunk failed-at-home deserter
shipwreck a parliament
also not in the library
cetshwayo's
            beautiful people
dancing in long lines free feet
beat on earth
            a few more guns
            already the principles
of fire control
            a few more
guns would have done the job

the king of the Goths who no longer dissembled his
appetite for plunder & revenge appeared in arms under
the walls of the capital; and the trembling senate,
without any hopes of relief, prepared by a desperate
resistance to delay the ruin of the country. But they
were unable to guard against the secret conspiracy of
their slaves and domestics, who either from birth or
interest were attached to the cause of the enemy. At
the hour of midnight the Salarian gate was silently
opened, and the inhabitants were awakened by the
tremendous sound of the Gothic trumpet. Eleven hundred
and sixty three years after the foundation of Rome,
the Imperial City, which had subdued and civilized
so considerable a part of mankind, was delivered to
the licentious fury of the tribes of Germany and Scythia.

August 24, 410 A.D.

IN THE CAPABILITY

of one man's breath
as marion as strings
shape vibrations in air
& memory

on purpose
a music which fights
environment rings phone rings
cash register clench yr teeth

close yr eyes you have
to hear the bass

up tight for
this or that good sounds do
not good vibrations make

hard ass city

st marks place 19 67
ornette patted joshua on the belly
& said "hey man"

A POEM CALLED SMOG

the constellations under which
i have been born have
not been described
water best gold burning fire
among man proud riches all matter expands
away from all other

we erect these
these rooms
in which we move
on 2nd ave
the phone rings

        the real
all around us

       because our ancestors
were slaves were brought forth
"with a strong hand

          no problems
are real in the sense
we think they are real best
never to have been born yet
honor dionysus honor
the bloody pieces roar
like a bull on the mountains

THE BROKEN LINE

ARE THE BIRDS
                TO THE QUIET ISLAND
for chrissake what
                can one say
to these people i
                have forgotten all that i know
i'm at a loss
          in the o
of utteranceo
                americans in me you
                              were believed
i wldve floated you
                a monument less durable
than brass

parturiunt montes
                the renaissance predicted
for chrissake
          what can you say

ANSWER ENOUGH

my friends have moved to
the ny times poetry
chicago airplanes
uncool their lives go
where they want em to

someone is waiting outside for
someone leave together walk
on the main street who here
has a grudge carries a blade

LITTLE CAESAR

the moral in a day when the word
had senses that you cannot quit
the reality of affection every
man's wife every woman's husband

THE OATH

I will kill by word and by deed and by my vote and with my own hand, if I am at all able, whosoever shall overthrow the democracy at Athens, and whosoever shall hold any public office after the overthrow of the democracy, and whosoever shall establish a tyranny, and whosoever shall help to establish a tyrant; and if someone else shall kill one of these, I shall consider him holy in the eyes of the gods and the divine powers, as having killed an enemy of the Athenians; and I shall sell all the property of the dead man and give half to the killer and I shall hold nothing back. If somebody dies while killing or trying to kill one of these, I will treat him with the kindness which was shown to Harmodius and Aristogeiton and their descendants. And all oaths, sworn at Athens or in the army camp or anywhere else against the people of Athens, I hereby abolish and renounce.

All the Athenians shall swear to this, over unblemished sacrifices, in the legal form, before the festival of Dionysus; and they shall pray for prosperity for he who keeps it, but for he who breaks it, destruction for him and for his whole family.

THE BEAUTIFUL PLANET

a song to make the scalp wrinkle
we have found an
anthem we shall
overcome

the rednecks ride by in cars
we stand on the church porch in the morning cold
hold hands we
are not afraid

all rise apartment houses
by the seashore red smoke
the pismo clam is on our side how
can we lose the redwoods & the lizards
are on our side our fear
in the present courage
out lasts clouds
how can we lose

we have an anthem a song hung
up on the wall of the temple
dripping to show we were
saved we have songs for
every occasion the axes
are on our side how can
we lose

WHEN TO THEE

seasons
sweat
silent
thought
eye
   (some on ups)

past new woes
past fourteenth street

the real is more beautiful
than the unreal
not because it is more real
but because it is more beautiful

regis debray
squinting into the lights
trying to say what he wants to
in a language he doesnt know too well

if i had the wings of an angel
what i would do would be an integral and necessary part
of the revolutionary struggle

thirty

let the forest
join us
brother tree
let us march brother grass

i am the 1st post american poet
broken into pieces to the
barricades shoot my father

no revolutionaries
corned beef & buttered
balls the lines

of this poem are not imaginary
the before mentioned discovery
of a new continent which i shall call

america in memory of

music